KINGDOM COMMERCE:
A Devotional Guide for Trucking Entrepreneurs

PART III: SUSTAINING SUCCESS AND GIVING BACK

"Sustaining Success and Giving Back" is the third and final part in this unique three-part devotional series created for those seeking a fresh start—especially individuals rebuilding their lives after incarceration, as well as those stepping into a new career path. This volume emphasizes maintaining balance, leading with ethics, and developing a business that positively influences the community. It offers guidance on creating a sustainable life and business while giving back, reminding readers that a faith-driven business is one that serves others. With scripture, reflection, and practical tools, *"Sustaining Success and Giving Back"* supports those who want not just to succeed, but to transform their past into a legacy of hope, integrity, and meaningful impact.

KINGDOM COMMERCE:
A Devotional Guide for Trucking Entrepreneurs

Part III: Sustaining Success and Giving Back

By Rodney E. Jackson, Box Truck 365

Copyright © 2024 BOXTRUCK365.com
ISBN 9798300011475

Printed in the United States of America.

All rights reserved. This book or any portion thereof may not be reproduced or used in any manner whatsoever without the express written permission of the publisher except for the use of brief quotations in a book review.

All Scripture quotations, unless otherwise indicated, are taken from the Holy Bible, New International Version®, NIV®. Copyright ©1973, 1978, 1984, 2011 by Biblica, Inc.™ Used by permission of Zondervan. All rights reserved worldwide. www.zondervan.com The "NIV" and "New International Version" are trademarks registered in the United States Patent and Trademark Office by Biblica, Inc.™.

Published by Meshelfies Books and Print
P O Box 660, Lancaster, TX 75146

MESHELFIES BOOKS
DALLAS, TEXAS

2 3 4 5 6 7 8 9 0 1

*In Loving Memory of Mr. Joe,
a mentor and friend*

PART III: SUSTAINING SUCCESS AND GIVING BACK 1

Maintaining Work-Life Balance 9
- Prioritizing Family 10
- Setting Boundaries 12
- Personal Health and Wellness 14
- Spiritual Growth 16
- Time for Recreation and Relaxation 18
- Managing Stress 20
- Weekly Reflection and Prayer 22

Ethical Business Practices 25
- Integrity in Business 26
- Fair Treatment of Employees 28
- Honesty with Clients 30
- Social Responsibility 32
- Environmental Stewardship 34
- Accountability 36
- Grace and Forgiveness 38

Giving Back and Community Involvement 41
- The Joy of Giving 42
- Supporting Local Communities 44
- Volunteering Time and Resources 46
- Mentoring Others 48
- Partnerships with Nonprofits 50
- Being a Light in the Marketplace 52
- Reflection and Thanksgiving 54

Sustaining Long-Term Success 57
- Vision for the Future 58
- Setting Long-Term Goals 60
- Adapting to Change 62
- Continual Learning and Growth 64
- Building a Legacy 66
- Celebrating Milestones 68
- Staying Drug-Free and Focused 70

Reflection and Commitment 73
- Reflecting on God's Faithfulness 74
- Renewing Your Commitment to God 76
- Embracing God's Call 78

Surrendering Your Will 80
Seeking God's Guidance Daily 82
Staying Faithful in Small Things.. 84
Living with an Eternal Perspective...................................... 86

FOREWORD

Years into the journey with Rodney's business, we reached a place of stability—a place where we could finally think beyond ourselves. With God's favor, the company had grown, and we found ourselves in a position to give back, blessing others as we had been blessed. *Sustaining Success and Giving Back* is all about reaching that next level, where your business becomes not just a source of income, but a source of impact.

We serve a God of abundance, who is capable of doing the impossible. But He also calls us to act with discernment, wisdom, and compassion. True success isn't just about what we gain; it's about what we give and the legacy we leave behind. In this volume, you'll find guidance on maintaining a balanced, ethical, and faith-centered approach to long-term success.

As you read, our prayer is that the Holy Spirit will inspire you to use your business as a means of blessing others. May God give you the wisdom to sustain success, the generosity to give freely, and the discernment to stay grounded in His Word. Remember, your business can be a testimony of God's faithfulness, making a difference in the lives of those you serve.

Maintaining Work-Life Balance

Prioritizing Family

"Children, obey your parents in the Lord, for this is right. 'Honor your father and mother' – which is the first commandment with a promise." – Ephesians 6:1-2

Balancing work and family life can be challenging, especially when you're passionate about your business. But family is one of God's greatest gifts, and making them a priority strengthens your relationships and gives you a supportive foundation. Honoring family commitments allows you to experience God's love in a different way and brings balance to a busy life.

- **Set Boundaries Between Work and Family Time**
  When it's time for family, be fully present. Try setting specific work hours and "off" hours to ensure that you can focus on your loved ones without distractions.

- **Plan Regular Family Activities**
  Create special moments by planning time with your family, whether it's a meal

together, a weekly game night, or an outing. These activities strengthen bonds and create lasting memories.

- **Encourage Open Communication**
  Make sure family members feel heard and valued. Listening to each other helps build trust and keeps you connected, even when work demands are high.

- **Involve Family in Your Business Journey**
  Share your goals, challenges, and successes with your family, so they feel part of your journey. This helps them understand why you're working hard and strengthens their support.

- **Pray for Wisdom in Prioritizing Your Family**
  Ask God to help you find the right balance between work and family. Pray for guidance to make decisions that honor both your family commitments and your business goals.

Dear God, thank You for the gift of family. Help me to make them a priority and to be fully present with them. Show me how to balance my time and energy between work and family, honoring both in a way that pleases You.
In Jesus' Name, Amen.

Setting Boundaries

"Then, because so many people were coming and going that they did not even have a chance to eat, he said to them, 'Come with me by yourselves to a quiet place and get some rest.'" – Mark 6:31

In a world that's always "on," setting boundaries is essential for maintaining a healthy work-life balance. Jesus recognized the need for rest, encouraging His disciples to step away from the busyness and recharge. Setting boundaries protects your well-being and helps you be more effective in all areas of life.

- **Schedule Breaks to Recharge**
  Just as Jesus took time to rest, you should too. Schedule regular breaks to avoid burnout and restore your energy.

- **Learn to Say No**
  It's okay to turn down requests or projects that would overload your schedule. Saying no helps you protect your time and energy for things that matter most.

- **Define Clear Work Hours**
  Set specific work hours and communicate them to others. By establishing clear boundaries, you can focus on work during work hours and be fully present outside of them.

- **Create a Physical Separation Between Work and Home**
  If possible, designate a specific area for work and leave it when you're done for the day. This physical separation can help you shift your mindset from work mode to personal time.

- **Pray for Strength to Uphold Boundaries**
  Ask God for the strength to set and maintain healthy boundaries. Pray that He'll guide you to make choices that honor your well-being and allow you to serve effectively.

Dear God, thank You for the wisdom of boundaries. Help me to recognize when I need to step back and rest, and give me the courage to set limits that protect my health and well-being. May I find strength and peace in following Your example of rest.
In Jesus' Name, Amen.

Personal Health and Wellness

"Do you not know that your bodies are temples of the Holy Spirit, who is in you, whom you have received from God? You are not your own." – 1 Corinthians 6:19

Caring for your body is part of honoring God, as He has given you the gift of health to serve Him well. Prioritizing wellness—physically, mentally, and spiritually—enhances your ability to carry out your purpose. When you prioritize your health, you're better equipped to face life's demands with energy and resilience.

- **Commit to Regular Exercise**
  Physical activity keeps your body strong and your mind sharp. Aim for consistent exercise, whether it's a daily walk, workout, or a fun physical activity you enjoy.

- **Nourish Your Body with Healthy Foods**
  Eating nutritious foods fuels your body and supports long-term health. Make mindful choices that provide the energy you need to stay focused and effective.

- **Practice Mental Wellness**
  Take steps to manage stress and nurture your mental health, whether through prayer, meditation, journaling, or connecting with loved ones.

- **Get Adequate Rest**
  Rest is essential for recovery and renewal. Prioritize sleep and regular downtime to ensure you have the energy to meet daily challenges.

- **Pray for a Healthy Mind, Body, and Spirit**
  Ask God to help you care for your health as a way to honor Him. Pray for discipline and wisdom in making choices that support your wellness.

Dear God, thank You for the gift of health. Help me to honor You by taking care of my body, mind, and spirit. Guide me in making choices that nourish and strengthen me, so I can serve You with my best self. In Jesus' Name, Amen.

Spiritual Growth

"But grow in the grace and knowledge of our Lord and Savior Jesus Christ. To him be glory both now and forever! Amen." – 2 Peter 3:18

Your relationship with God is the foundation of everything you do. Growing spiritually allows you to deepen that connection, find purpose, and experience His presence more fully. Spiritual growth is a lifelong journey that strengthens your faith and keeps you aligned with God's will.

- **Spend Time Daily in God's Word**
  Reading the Bible daily nurtures your faith and provides wisdom for life. Make it a habit to seek God's guidance through His Word.

- **Pray Regularly to Deepen Your Connection with God**
  Consistent prayer strengthens your relationship with God. Talk with Him throughout the day, sharing your thoughts, worries, and gratitude.

- **Reflect on God's Work in Your Life**
  Take time to reflect on how God has been working in your life. Gratitude and reflection deepen your awareness of His presence and blessings.

- **Seek Fellowship with Other Believers**
  Surrounding yourself with other believers encourages growth and accountability. Join a small group or find a church community where you can share faith and encourage one another.

- **Pray for a Heart Open to Spiritual Growth**
  Ask God to guide you on your journey of growth. Pray for a teachable spirit and a desire to grow closer to Him each day.

Dear God, thank You for calling me to grow in grace and knowledge of You. Help me to seek You daily and to deepen my relationship with You. Open my heart to spiritual growth, and guide me on this journey of faith. In Jesus' Name, Amen.

Time for Recreation and Relaxation

"I know that there is nothing better for people than to be happy and to do good while they live. That each of them may eat and drink, and find satisfaction in all their toil – this is the gift of God." – Ecclesiastes 3:12-13

God desires that we find joy in life, even amid our work and responsibilities. Taking time to relax and enjoy recreation is not only refreshing but also a gift from God. When we rest, we recharge and reconnect with Him, allowing us to return to our work with renewed energy and purpose.

- **Schedule Regular Breaks for Rest**
  Incorporate breaks into your schedule, allowing yourself time to relax and unwind. Even short breaks can help clear your mind and reduce stress.

- **Engage in Activities That Bring You Joy**
  Recreation and leisure activities, whether it's a hobby, sport, or time in nature, help restore your energy. Find activities that

bring you joy and make them part of your life.

- **Spend Quality Time with Loved Ones**
Relationships are an important part of recreation and relaxation. Enjoying time with friends and family helps strengthen bonds and creates lasting memories.

- **Practice Mindfulness in Your Free Time**
Focus on being present during your moments of rest. Practicing mindfulness helps you fully enjoy each experience, bringing peace and clarity.

- **Pray for a Balanced Heart in Work and Leisure**
Ask God to help you find balance between work and rest. Pray for a heart that enjoys both work and relaxation, honoring Him in all areas of your life.

Dear God, thank You for the gift of rest and recreation. Help me to embrace moments of relaxation and to find joy in activities that bring refreshment. Teach me to balance work and leisure, so I can serve You with a renewed heart.
In Jesus' Name, Amen.

Managing Stress

"Cast your cares on the Lord and he will sustain you; he will never let the righteous be shaken." – Psalm 55:22

Stress is a reality of life, especially when balancing work and personal commitments. But God invites us to cast our cares on Him, trusting that He will sustain us. Learning to manage stress helps you approach each day with peace and strength, knowing that God is with you through every challenge.

- **Identify Stressors and Address Them**
  Take time to identify what's causing stress in your life. Once you know your stressors, find practical ways to address or minimize them with God's help.

- **Practice Deep Breathing and Relaxation Techniques**
  Physical relaxation techniques, like deep breathing or meditation, can calm your mind and body. These practices help you

stay grounded and handle stress more effectively.

- **Create a Balanced Schedule**
  Overloading your schedule can increase stress. Set realistic goals for each day, and make sure you leave space for rest and reflection.

- **Lean on God Through Prayer**
  Talk to God about your stress and trust Him to handle your burdens. Regular prayer can reduce anxiety, reminding you that He is in control.

- **Pray for Peace and Strength**
  Ask God to help you manage stress and find peace in every situation. Pray for the strength to let go of worries and to trust Him completely.

Dear God, thank You for being my refuge in times of stress. Help me to manage my stress well and to cast my cares on You. Teach me to trust You with every burden, knowing that You will sustain me.
In Jesus' Name, Amen.

Weekly Reflection and Prayer

"Do not be anxious about anything, but in every situation, by prayer and petition, with thanksgiving, present your requests to God." – Philippians 4:6-7

Setting aside time each week to reflect and pray is a powerful practice for maintaining a balanced life. Reflection allows you to assess your week, celebrate victories, and learn from challenges. Through prayer, you can lay your concerns before God and find peace in His presence.

- **Take Time Each Week for Reflection**
  At the end of each week, spend time thinking about your experiences, successes, and areas for growth. Reflecting helps you gain insight and prepare for the week ahead.

- **Express Gratitude for the Week's Blessings**
  Remember to thank God for the blessings you received throughout the week.

Gratitude shifts your focus to the positive, filling your heart with peace and joy.

- **Bring Your Concerns to God in Prayer**
Use this time to lay your worries and struggles before God, trusting Him with everything. Prayer helps you release anxieties and find rest in His presence.

- **Seek God's Guidance for the Upcoming Week**
Ask God to guide your steps in the coming days. Pray for wisdom and strength to handle the responsibilities and challenges that lie ahead.

- **Pray for a Heart Attuned to God's Presence**
Ask God to keep you mindful of His presence throughout the week, helping you find peace in knowing that He is always with you.

Dear God, thank You for the opportunity to reflect and pray. Help me to bring all my concerns and gratitude to You, trusting in Your wisdom and guidance. Prepare my heart for the week ahead, and keep me attuned to Your presence every day.
In Jesus' Name, Amen.

ETHICAL BUSINESS PRACTICES

Integrity in Business

"The Lord detests dishonest scales, but accurate weights find favor with him." – Proverbs 11:1

Integrity is foundational to ethical business practices. Proverbs reminds us that God values honesty and fairness in all our dealings. Practicing integrity in business means honoring commitments, being truthful, and treating others with respect. It builds trust with customers, employees, and partners, and it brings honor to God.

- **Be Honest in All Transactions**
  Always communicate honestly with customers, partners, and employees. Avoid exaggerating or making promises you can't keep, as honesty strengthens trust and credibility.

- **Honor Commitments and Contracts**
  If you make a commitment, follow through on it. Keeping your word, even when it's difficult, demonstrates respect for others and reflects God's standards for integrity.

- **Treat Employees and Partners Fairly**
  Fair treatment in pay, recognition, and respect for others' contributions shows your commitment to ethical practices. This builds a positive reputation and a stronger team.

- **Avoid Cutting Corners**
  It may be tempting to cut corners to save time or money, but maintaining high standards reflects integrity. Choose to do things right, even if it's more challenging.

- **Pray for Strength to Maintain Integrity**
  Ask God for the courage to uphold integrity, especially when faced with difficult choices. Pray for wisdom to act ethically in every situation.

Dear God, thank You for being a God of truth and integrity. Help me to reflect Your character in my business dealings and to be honest, fair, and trustworthy in all I do. Give me strength to maintain integrity, even when it's hard.
In Jesus' Name, Amen.

Fair Treatment of Employees

"Masters, provide your slaves with what is right and fair, because you know that you also have a Master in heaven." – Colossians 4:1

Fair treatment of employees is essential for creating a positive, respectful workplace. Colossians reminds us that, just as God treats us with grace and fairness, we should do the same for those who work with us. Treating employees fairly not only improves morale but also reflects God's love and justice.

- **Value Each Employee's Contribution**
  Show appreciation for the efforts of your employees. Recognize their work and let them know they're valued; it builds loyalty and fosters a healthy work environment.

- **Provide Fair Compensation and Opportunities**
  Ensure that employees are paid fairly and have equal opportunities for growth and advancement. Treating employees fairly in

compensation and promotion demonstrates respect and fairness.

- **Create a Respectful and Inclusive Workplace**
  Foster an environment where everyone feels respected and included, regardless of their role or background. Treating each person with dignity is part of ethical business practices.

- **Listen to Employee Feedback**
  Take time to listen to employees' concerns or suggestions. Showing empathy and openness encourages trust and helps you grow as a leader.

- **Pray for Wisdom in Managing Your Team**
  Ask God for wisdom to lead with fairness, kindness, and respect. Pray that He'll help you see your employees as He does, and to treat them with His love and justice.

---

*Dear God, thank You for the people who work alongside me. Help me to treat each one with fairness and respect, valuing their contributions and providing them with opportunities to grow. May I lead with integrity, reflecting Your love in every interaction.
In Jesus' Name, Amen.*

Honesty with Clients

"The Lord detests lying lips, but he delights in people who are trustworthy." – Proverbs 12:22

Being honest with clients builds trust and strengthens relationships. Proverbs tells us that God delights in those who are trustworthy, and honesty is a key part of that. By being transparent and upfront, you create a reputation of reliability, encouraging clients to trust your services and refer you to others.

- **Communicate Clearly and Truthfully**
  Be transparent in your communications, providing accurate information about products, services, and pricing. Clear and honest communication fosters trust and prevents misunderstandings.

- **Address Mistakes Openly**
  If something goes wrong, be honest with the client about what happened and how you plan to fix it. Owning up to mistakes shows accountability and builds trust.

- **Avoid Misleading Promotions**
  Ensure that marketing materials and promotions accurately represent what you offer. Misleading promotions can damage your reputation and hinder trust with clients.

- **Follow Through on Promises**
  Make sure to deliver on any promises you make to clients. Following through on commitments strengthens your reputation as a trustworthy business.

- **Pray for Integrity in Client Relations**
  Ask God to guide you in building honest, trusting relationships with clients. Pray for the wisdom to be transparent in all interactions, honoring God through your work.

Dear God, thank You for the clients and customers You have entrusted to me. Help me to serve them with honesty and integrity, reflecting Your truth in all I do. May my words and actions build trust and honor You. In Jesus' Name, Amen.

Social Responsibility

"Whoever is kind to the poor lends to the Lord, and he will reward them for what they have done." – Proverbs 19:17

Social responsibility is an important aspect of ethical business practices. God calls us to show kindness and compassion to those in need, reminding us that our actions reflect His love. Being socially responsible means using your business to make a positive impact, helping to uplift others and serve your community.

- **Give Back to the Community**
  Find ways to support local initiatives, whether through donations, volunteer work, or partnerships. Giving back strengthens your community and reflects God's compassion.

- **Promote Sustainable Practices**
  Consider how your business can contribute to sustainability, reducing waste and environmental impact. Small steps can

make a big difference in caring for God's creation.

- **Support Charitable Causes**
  Partner with organizations or causes that align with your values. Supporting charitable efforts allows your business to contribute to broader social good.

- **Foster a Culture of Kindness and Service**
  Encourage kindness and service within your team. When employees see social responsibility as part of your business's values, it builds a positive culture.

- **Pray for a Heart of Compassion**
  Ask God to help you see opportunities to make a difference. Pray for a compassionate heart that seeks to serve others, using your business to bring hope and help.

Dear God, thank You for the resources and opportunities You've given me. Help me to use them responsibly, showing kindness to those in need and serving my community well. Give me a heart of compassion, and guide me in making choices that reflect Your love.
In Jesus' Name, Amen.

Environmental Stewardship

"The Lord God took the man and put him in the Garden of Eden to work it and take care of it." – Genesis 2:15

God has entrusted us with the earth, calling us to be good stewards of His creation. Environmental stewardship is about caring for the resources we've been given and making sustainable choices in business that honor God's creation. Small actions in how we run our businesses can make a positive impact on the environment and show respect for the earth He made.

- **Reduce Waste in Daily Operations**
  Look for ways to minimize waste, whether through recycling, reducing packaging, or using eco-friendly materials. Small steps add up and reflect a commitment to environmental stewardship.

- **Conserve Energy Where Possible**
  Using energy-efficient equipment and turning off unused electronics can reduce your business's energy footprint. These

practices are good for the planet and often save on costs.

- **Source Sustainable Materials**
  If your business requires materials, seek sustainable options where possible. This shows respect for natural resources and demonstrates a long-term approach to caring for the earth.

- **Educate Your Team on Environmental Responsibility**
  Encourage your employees to adopt environmentally friendly practices. When everyone is aware of the importance of stewardship, it creates a positive culture of care for creation.

- **Pray for Wisdom in Environmental Stewardship**
  Ask God for guidance on how to make your business practices more sustainable. Pray for creativity in finding ways to reduce your environmental impact while honoring Him.

---

*Dear God, thank You for entrusting me with the earth and its resources. Help me to be a good steward in my business, making choices that honor Your creation. Guide me to use resources wisely and to care for the environment in ways that bring glory to You.
In Jesus' Name, Amen.*

Accountability

"Now it is required that those who have been given a trust must prove faithful." – 1 Corinthians 4:2

Accountability is essential in business, helping you to remain faithful to your values and commitments. Whether it's financial integrity, ethical decision-making, or staying true to your mission, being accountable means you take responsibility for your actions. Accountability builds trust and strengthens your reputation as a reliable, trustworthy leader.

- **Stay Transparent in Financial Matters**
  Honesty in finances is crucial for accountability. Keep accurate records, avoid shortcuts, and ensure that all transactions are conducted with integrity.

- **Seek Accountability Partners**
  Surround yourself with people who encourage you to stay true to your values. Trusted advisors, mentors, or partners can

offer perspective and help you make wise decisions.

- **Create a Culture of Accountability**
  Encourage accountability among your team by setting clear expectations and following up on commitments. When everyone understands their responsibilities, it builds trust and consistency.

- **Regularly Review Your Goals and Progress**
  Take time to assess your goals and ensure you're on track. Regular check-ins help you stay aligned with your mission and make necessary adjustments.

- **Pray for Integrity in All Actions**
  Ask God to help you remain faithful in all areas of your business. Pray for the courage to be transparent and for the wisdom to handle accountability well.

Dear God, thank You for entrusting me with responsibilities. Help me to remain accountable in all I do, reflecting honesty and integrity in my work. Guide me to make wise decisions and to honor the trust You have placed in me.
In Jesus' Name, Amen.

Grace and Forgiveness

"Be kind and compassionate to one another, forgiving each other, just as in Christ God forgave you."
– Ephesians 4:32

Running a business can be challenging—mistakes happen, conflicts arise, and the pressure to succeed can weigh heavily. In these moments, grace and forgiveness are essential. Grace means offering kindness and understanding, even when it's undeserved. Forgiveness allows you to move forward, rebuild trust, and demonstrate God's love in action.

Here's how you can practice grace and forgiveness in your business:

- **Show kindness in correction**: When an employee makes a mistake, respond with patience. Use the moment to teach and encourage rather than react with frustration.

- **Reconcile relationships**: Conflicts with clients or team members happen. Be quick

to forgive and seek peace, fostering stronger connections and mutual respect.
- **Forgive yourself**: When you fall short, trust in God's mercy and let go of self-blame. Accept His grace to renew your focus and keep moving forward.

Extending grace and forgiveness not only reflects Christ in your leadership but also creates a culture of growth, trust, and restoration in your workplace.

Dear God, thank You for showing me grace and forgiveness through Your love. Help me to lead with compassion and understanding in my business. Teach me to forgive others as You have forgiven me, and remind me to accept Your grace when I fall short. Let my actions inspire trust, healing, and growth in those I serve.
In Jesus' Name, Amen.

GIVING BACK AND COMMUNITY INVOLVEMENT

The Joy of Giving

"Each of you should give what you have decided in your heart to give, not reluctantly or under compulsion, for God loves a cheerful giver."
– 2 Corinthians 9:7

Giving back to others is a core part of living out your faith and building a meaningful legacy. The joy of giving goes beyond any material benefit—it's a blessing for both the giver and the receiver. When we give cheerfully, we reflect God's generous heart and experience the joy that comes from selflessness.

- **Give with a Willing Heart**
  Rather than feeling pressured, give out of a genuine desire to help others. A willing heart reflects God's love and brings joy to both you and those you help.

- **Find Ways to Serve in Your Community**
  Look for opportunities to support your community, whether through volunteer work, donations, or mentorship. Engaging

locally builds connections and strengthens community bonds.

- **Encourage a Culture of Giving in Your Business**
Inspire your team to embrace giving by setting an example. When your business values generosity, it becomes a place where kindness thrives.

- **Give Consistently, Not Just When Convenient**
Make giving a regular part of your life. Whether big or small, consistent acts of kindness show a steady commitment to helping others.

- **Pray for a Joyful Heart in Giving**
Ask God to help you give freely and joyfully. Pray that your generosity would be a reflection of His love and a source of hope to others.

Dear God, thank You for the joy that comes from giving. Help me to give with a cheerful heart, freely and without hesitation. May my actions reflect Your love and inspire others to share generously.
In Jesus' Name, Amen.

Supporting Local Communities

"Give, and it will be given to you. A good measure, pressed down, shaken together and running over, will be poured into your lap. For with the measure you use, it will be measured to you." – Luke 6:38

Supporting local communities is a meaningful way to contribute to God's work beyond our own lives. Investing in the needs around you allows you to give back to the people and places that shape your business. When you support others, you create a positive ripple effect that blesses your community and, in turn, brings blessings back to you.

- **Partner with Local Organizations**
  Collaborate with nonprofits, schools, or other community organizations to address local needs. Partnerships help create lasting change and build a stronger community.

- **Use Your Business to Make a Positive Impact**
  Look for ways your business can

contribute, whether through donating products, hosting events, or offering services that benefit the community.

- **Encourage Employees to Get Involved**
  Invite your team to participate in community efforts. Group activities, like volunteering or organizing fundraisers, strengthen team bonds and show that your business values giving back.

- **Celebrate and Support Other Local Businesses**
  Show appreciation for local businesses by supporting and promoting them. A strong local network benefits everyone and reinforces a spirit of community.

- **Pray for Wisdom in Supporting Your Community**
  Ask God to guide you in identifying areas where you can make a meaningful impact. Pray for the resources and wisdom to serve your community well.

Dear God, thank You for the blessing of community. Help me to give back and support those around me in ways that make a positive impact. Guide me in using my business to serve and strengthen my community.
In Jesus' Name, Amen.

Volunteering Time and Resources

"Each of you should use whatever gift you have received to serve others, as faithful stewards of God's grace in its various forms." – 1 Peter 4:10

God has blessed each of us with unique gifts, and volunteering is a powerful way to use those gifts for His purpose. By dedicating your time and resources to serve others, you're able to give back in ways that extend beyond financial support. Volunteering allows you to be the hands and feet of Christ, showing His love through service.

- **Identify Your Strengths and Talents**
  Reflect on the skills and resources God has given you. Use these gifts to serve others in ways that make a real difference.

- **Dedicate Time to Serve Regularly**
  Set aside time on a regular basis to volunteer, whether it's at a local organization, church, or community event.

Consistent service shows commitment and helps you build relationships.

- **Encourage Team Involvement in Service Projects**
  Organize volunteer opportunities for your employees or team. Serving together builds a sense of unity and reinforces the importance of giving back.

- **Consider Offering Pro Bono Services**
  If you have a service-oriented business, consider providing services free of charge to those in need. This is a practical way to bless others and use your resources for good.

- **Pray for a Heart of Service**
  Ask God to help you see opportunities to serve others and to give you a heart that delights in helping those in need.

Dear God, thank You for the gifts You have given me. Help me to use them in ways that serve others and bring glory to Your name. Give me a heart that finds joy in volunteering and a willingness to give freely of my time and resources.
In Jesus' Name, Amen.

Mentoring Others

"Similarly, encourage the young men to be self-controlled. In everything set them an example by doing what is good. In your teaching show integrity, seriousness." – Titus 2:6-7

Mentorship is a powerful way to pass on knowledge, wisdom, and faith to others. Through mentorship, you can help guide others on their journeys, offering support and encouragement as they navigate life and work. Mentoring isn't just about teaching skills; it's about setting a Christ-like example and building relationships that inspire growth.

- **Share Your Experiences to Help Others Grow**
  Be open about your own journey, including the successes and challenges you've faced. Your experiences can provide valuable insight and encouragement.

- **Be a Consistent and Reliable Presence**
  Consistency is key in mentorship. Show up

regularly for those you mentor, offering steady support and guidance as they navigate their path.

- **Encourage Personal and Professional Development**
  Help those you mentor set goals, both in their personal and professional lives. Encouraging growth in all areas demonstrates a holistic approach to mentorship.

- **Lead by Example**
  Show integrity and faith in your own life. By living out the values you hope to pass on, you provide a model that others can look up to and follow.

- **Pray for Guidance in Mentorship**
  Ask God to guide you in your mentorship, giving you the wisdom to support and encourage others effectively.

Dear God, thank You for the opportunity to mentor others. Help me to be a positive influence and a steady source of support. Guide me in setting a Christ-like example and offering encouragement to those who are growing in their journeys.
In Jesus' Name, Amen.

Partnerships with Nonprofits

"The generous will themselves be blessed, for they share their food with the poor." – Proverbs 22:9

Partnering with nonprofits allows you to contribute to a greater cause, combining resources and efforts to make a lasting impact. Nonprofits often focus on specific needs within communities, making them valuable partners in serving others. By forming partnerships, your business can contribute to meaningful work and help reach those in need.

- **Identify Nonprofits Aligned with Your Values**
  Seek out organizations whose missions align with your values and vision. This ensures that your partnership is meaningful and reinforces the principles you want to promote.

- **Offer Support Through Donations or Services**
  Whether through financial contributions or in-kind services, find ways to support these

organizations. Your contributions help them continue their work and extend their reach.

- **Promote the Partnership to Raise Awareness**
Use your business platform to spread the word about the nonprofits you support. Raising awareness encourages others to get involved and shows your commitment to community impact.

- **Involve Employees in Partnership Efforts**
Invite your team to participate in partnership activities, such as volunteer events or fundraising campaigns. This builds team unity and demonstrates a commitment to giving back.

- **Pray for Impactful Partnerships**
Ask God to guide you in forming partnerships that make a real difference. Pray for wisdom to support nonprofits in meaningful ways and for a spirit of generosity in all your interactions.

Dear God, thank You for the opportunity to partner with organizations that serve others. Help me to support these nonprofits in meaningful ways, using my resources to extend Your love and kindness. Guide me in building partnerships that bring hope and make a lasting impact.
In Jesus' Name, Amen.

Being a Light in the Marketplace

"In the same way, let your light shine before others, that they may see your good deeds and glorify your Father in heaven." – Matthew 5:16

As believers, we are called to be a light in the world, reflecting God's love and goodness wherever we go—including the workplace. Being a light in the marketplace means conducting business in a way that honors God and serves as a positive example to others. Through integrity, kindness, and service, you can show God's love to customers, employees, and partners.

- **Show Kindness and Respect in All Interactions**
  Treat everyone—customers, employees, and competitors—with kindness and respect. Your actions reflect God's love and create a positive work environment.
- **Stand Firm in Your Values**
  Even when it's difficult, stay true to your

values. Integrity in business decisions demonstrates strength and sets an example for others to follow.
- **Use Your Business to Serve Others**
Look for ways to make a positive impact, whether through customer service, fair treatment of employees, or community involvement. Serving others reflects God's love and makes your business a light in the community.
- **Encourage a Culture of Generosity and Support**
Promote a culture that values generosity and support within your business. When employees see a positive environment, they are more likely to embrace and reflect these values.
- **Pray to Shine God's Light**
Ask God to help you be a light in the marketplace, bringing hope and encouragement to others. Pray for strength to live out your faith in your business and to inspire others to seek God.

Dear God, thank You for the opportunity to be a light in the marketplace. Help me to reflect Your love and truth in all my business interactions, showing kindness, integrity, and generosity. May my actions point others to You and bring glory to Your name.
In Jesus' Name, Amen.

Reflection and Thanksgiving

"Let the peace of Christ rule in your hearts, since as members of one body you were called to peace. And be thankful." – Colossians 3:15

Taking time for reflection and thanksgiving helps you recognize God's blessings and express gratitude for His faithfulness. In business and in life, remembering what God has done brings peace, humbles your heart, and strengthens your relationship with Him. A thankful heart also creates a positive mindset that impacts everyone around you.

- **Reflect Regularly on God's Faithfulness**
  Set aside time to think about how God has blessed you and your business. Reflection on His faithfulness brings peace and perspective, especially during challenging times.

- **Celebrate Milestones and Achievements**
  Recognize the progress you've made, big or small, and give thanks for each

achievement. Celebrating milestones helps you see God's hand at work in every step of the journey.

- **Express Gratitude to Those Around You**
  Show appreciation for the people who have supported you—family, friends, employees, and customers. A simple thank-you goes a long way in building positive relationships.

- **Keep a Gratitude Journal**
  Writing down things you're grateful for each day helps you focus on the positive and reinforces a thankful attitude. Over time, it serves as a reminder of God's continuous blessings.

- **Pray with a Heart of Thanksgiving**
  Thank God for His guidance, provision, and grace. Ask Him to help you remain humble and grateful, no matter what circumstances arise.

Dear God, thank You for Your faithfulness in my life and my business. Help me to reflect on Your goodness and to keep a thankful heart in every situation. May I celebrate each blessing and share my gratitude with others, honoring You in all I do.
In Jesus' Name, Amen.

SUSTAINING LONG-TERM SUCCESS

Vision for the Future

"In their hearts humans plan their course, but the Lord establishes their steps." – Proverbs 16:9

Building a successful, long-lasting business requires vision, yet it's essential to remember that our plans are best grounded in God's guidance. Proverbs reminds us that while we may envision a direction for our lives and work, God ultimately establishes our steps. Trusting Him to guide our future brings peace and assurance that we're on the right path.

- **Set Clear Goals with God in Mind**
  Create goals that align with God's values and purpose. Think about where you'd like your business to be in the coming years, but be open to the ways God might shape those goals.

- **Pray for Direction and Discernment**
  Seek God's guidance for every plan you make. Regular prayer for wisdom and

discernment keeps your vision aligned with His will.

- **Remain Flexible to God's Leading**
  While it's good to have a plan, be willing to adjust as God directs. Trust that He may change your path to bring about something even greater than you imagined.

- **Visualize Your Impact, Not Just Your Success**
  Focus on the impact you want your business to have—on your employees, customers, and community. A vision focused on service, rather than just profit, honors God's purpose.

- **Pray for God's Blessing on Your Vision**
  Ask God to bless your vision and to help you see it through. Pray for faithfulness in following His leading every step of the way.

Dear God, thank You for guiding me as I plan for the future. Help me to set goals that honor You and align with Your purpose. Lead me each step of the way, establishing my steps and giving me the courage to follow Your path.
In Jesus' Name, Amen.

Setting Long-Term Goals

"I have fought the good fight, I have finished the race, I have kept the faith." – 2 Timothy 4:7

Setting long-term goals is like preparing for a marathon rather than a sprint. Success over time requires persistence, dedication, and a strong foundation. As Paul describes in 2 Timothy, faithfulness to the end is what truly counts. In your business, setting sustainable goals keeps you focused on the journey, not just the destination.

- **Break Down Goals into Achievable Steps**
  Create a roadmap with small, manageable steps. Each step brings you closer to your long-term goals, helping you stay motivated and focused.

- **Keep Your Goals Aligned with Your Values**
  Make sure your long-term goals reflect God's values. Success rooted in integrity and purpose will stand the test of time.

- **Stay Persistent, Even When Progress Is Slow**
  Success doesn't always come quickly. Be patient and keep pressing forward, trusting that God honors perseverance and faithfulness.

- **Review and Adjust Goals Regularly**
  Check in on your progress and make adjustments as needed. Staying adaptable allows you to respond to new opportunities and challenges along the way.

- **Pray for Strength to Stay the Course**
  Ask God to give you the endurance and determination to keep moving toward your goals. Pray for faith to finish the race well, trusting in His timing and provision.

Dear God, thank You for the strength and perseverance to pursue long-term goals. Help me to keep my focus on what truly matters and to stay faithful in every step. May my efforts honor You, and may I complete the work You've set before me.
In Jesus' Name, Amen.

Adapting to Change

"But those who hope in the Lord will renew their strength. They will soar on wings like eagles; they will run and not grow weary, they will walk and not be faint." – Isaiah 40:31

Change is inevitable, especially in business. The ability to adapt and grow through change is essential for long-term success. Isaiah reminds us that those who hope in the Lord will find renewed strength to face whatever comes their way. Trusting God in times of change allows us to remain steady and confident.

- **Embrace Change as Part of Growth**
  Change is often uncomfortable, but it can lead to growth and new opportunities. Be open to change as a way for God to bring about positive transformation.

- **Stay Grounded in Your Core Values**
  In times of change, hold onto your values. Remaining rooted in your beliefs provides

stability even when the circumstances around you shift.

- **Seek God's Guidance in Every Transition**
  When facing change, ask God for wisdom to make the best decisions. His guidance brings clarity and peace as you navigate new challenges.

- **Find Strength in Community**
  Lean on trusted mentors, friends, and employees during periods of change. Having a support system helps you adapt more confidently.

- **Pray for Courage to Embrace Change**
  Ask God for the courage to face change head-on and the resilience to adapt. Pray that you'll find renewed strength and hope in Him, trusting in His plan.

Dear God, thank You for being my anchor through times of change. Help me to embrace change as part of Your plan and to find strength in You. Give me courage, wisdom, and confidence as I move forward.
In Jesus' Name, Amen.

Continual Learning and Growth

"Let the wise listen and add to their learning, and let the discerning get guidance." – Proverbs 1:5

Learning and growth are essential for sustained success, both in business and in faith. Proverbs encourages us to continually seek knowledge and wisdom. Embracing a mindset of lifelong learning allows you to adapt, improve, and keep your business aligned with God's purpose.

- **Commit to Ongoing Education and Skill Development**
  Make it a priority to learn new skills or deepen your knowledge. Staying current in your field helps you lead effectively and make informed decisions.

- **Stay Humble and Open to Feedback**
  Be willing to learn from others, whether it's employees, mentors, or peers. Humility in receiving feedback opens the door to personal and professional growth.

- **Study God's Word for Guidance**
  Regularly read scripture for insight and direction. God's Word offers wisdom that applies to every aspect of life and work.

- **Encourage Growth in Your Team**
  Support and encourage learning within your team. Providing opportunities for development fosters a culture of growth and excellence.

- **Pray for a Teachable Spirit**
  Ask God to give you a heart that's open to learning. Pray for the wisdom to grow in knowledge and understanding, always seeking His guidance.

Dear God, thank You for the gift of growth and learning. Help me to remain teachable and open to new insights. Guide me as I continue to develop skills and knowledge that honor You and serve others.
In Jesus' Name, Amen.

Building a Legacy

"Blessed are those who fear the Lord, who find great delight in his commands. Their children will be mighty in the land; the generation of the upright will be blessed." – Psalm 112:1-2

A true legacy is built not just on achievements or wealth, but on faith, integrity, and the positive impact left for future generations. Psalm 112 reminds us that when we honor God, the blessings can flow to those who come after us. Building a legacy means living in a way that reflects God's love and principles, ensuring that our influence continues long after we're gone.

- **Live by Example**
  Set an example of integrity, kindness, and dedication. Your actions speak louder than words and can inspire others, especially those close to you.

- **Invest in Relationships**
  The people around you—family, friends, employees—are a crucial part of your

legacy. Show love and invest in their growth, supporting them in their journeys.

- **Focus on Character Over Success**
  Legacy is more about who you are than what you've achieved. Aim to build a life marked by godly character, humility, and service.

- **Mentor and Guide Others**
  Be intentional about sharing wisdom and experience. Mentorship allows you to pass down valuable lessons that will benefit others long after you're gone.

- **Pray for a Lasting Impact**
  Ask God to use your life as a positive influence and to help you create a legacy that reflects His goodness.

Dear God, thank You for the opportunity to build a legacy that honors You. Help me to live with integrity, to invest in those around me, and to leave a lasting impact that reflects Your love. May my life inspire others to follow You and live with purpose.
In Jesus' Name, Amen.

Celebrating Milestones

"Rejoice in the Lord always. I will say it again: Rejoice!" – Philippians 4:4

Milestones are important markers on our journey, reminding us of God's faithfulness and the progress we've made. Celebrating these moments isn't just about recognizing accomplishments; it's about giving thanks to God for His guidance and provision along the way. Taking time to celebrate keeps us motivated and grateful.

- **Acknowledge God's Role in Your Success**
  Recognize that each milestone is a result of God's hand in your life. Give thanks for His guidance and provision at every step.

- **Celebrate With Those Who Support You**
  Share your achievements with the people who've helped you along the way. Celebrating together builds stronger relationships and honors their role in your journey.

- **Reflect on Lessons Learned**
  Use milestones as a time to reflect on what you've learned and how you've grown. Each step is part of your journey, shaping you for what lies ahead.

- **Set New Goals**
  Celebrating milestones is also a great time to think about future goals. Reflect on your progress and set new, faith-driven objectives.

- **Pray With Gratitude**
  Take time to thank God in prayer for each milestone. A heart of gratitude keeps you focused on His blessings and strengthens your trust in Him.

Dear God, thank You for each milestone and for guiding me along this journey. Help me to celebrate with a heart full of gratitude, always recognizing Your presence and provision. May each milestone remind me of Your goodness and inspire me to continue growing. In Jesus' Name, Amen.

Staying Drug-Free and Focused

"Do you not know that your bodies are temples of the Holy Spirit, who is in you, whom you have received from God? You are not your own."
– 1 Corinthians 6:19

Remaining drug-free and staying focused are essential for building a successful life and business. God calls us to honor our bodies and to use them in ways that glorify Him. By choosing a lifestyle of clarity and focus, you protect your ability to serve God's purpose in your life, staying strong and equipped for the journey He has set before you.

- **Value Your Health as God's Gift**
  Recognize that your body is a gift from God, created to serve Him. Taking care of it through healthy choices honors Him and keeps you capable of doing His work.

- **Stay Committed to Clarity and Focus**
  Drugs or any harmful substances can cloud judgment and distract you from your goals. Staying focused enables you to be present and effective in all areas of your life.
- **Seek Support When Needed**
  Surround yourself with supportive people who encourage positive choices. Accountability and encouragement from friends, family, or mentors can make a significant difference.
- **Develop Healthy Habits to Relieve Stress**
  Find productive ways to cope with stress, such as prayer, exercise, or hobbies. Healthy outlets keep you balanced and focused without resorting to harmful substances.
- **Pray for Strength and Self-Control**
  Ask God for strength to remain drug-free and focused on His purpose for your life. Pray for the self-control needed to make choices that honor Him.

Dear God, thank You for the gift of health and for calling me to live a life that honors You. Help me to stay drug-free and focused on Your purpose. Give me the strength and self-control to make choices that reflect Your love and care for me.
In Jesus' Name, Amen.

REFLECTION AND COMMITMENT

Reflecting on God's Faithfulness

"Remember the wonders he has done, his miracles, and the judgments he pronounced." – Psalm 105:5

Taking time to reflect on God's faithfulness is an essential part of spiritual growth. Psalm 105:5 reminds us to remember the wonders and miracles God has done in our lives. When we reflect on His past faithfulness, we gain confidence in His presence and guidance in the future. This habit of reflection strengthens our relationship with God, deepens our gratitude, and renews our commitment to follow Him.

- **List the Ways God Has Been Faithful**
  Write down specific ways God has shown up in your life. This could be moments of answered prayers, unexpected blessings, or times of protection and guidance.

- **Share Your Testimony**
  Reflecting on God's faithfulness is powerful, but sharing it with others brings

encouragement and hope. Your testimony can strengthen someone else's faith and remind them of God's goodness.

- **Celebrate Small Victories**
  Sometimes God's faithfulness shows up in the little things. Don't overlook small victories — celebrate them as signs of His care and involvement in every aspect of your life.

- **Remember During Challenges**
  When facing hard times, remind yourself of how God has been faithful before. Trusting that He will be with you again provides peace and reassurance.

- **Pray for a Grateful Heart**
  Ask God to help you recognize His faithfulness daily. A heart of gratitude opens your eyes to His blessings, both big and small.

Dear God, thank You for Your unwavering faithfulness in my life. Help me to reflect on Your goodness and remember all the ways You've guided, protected, and blessed me. May my heart be filled with gratitude and my spirit renewed as I reflect on Your wonders.
In Jesus' Name, Amen.

Renewing Your Commitment to God

"Commit to the Lord whatever you do, and he will establish your plans." – Proverbs 16:3

Our relationship with God requires regular commitment, just as any relationship does. Proverbs 16:3 reminds us to commit all our ways to God, trusting Him to guide and establish our plans. When we renew our commitment to God, we choose to put Him at the center of our lives and invite Him to work through us.

- **Dedicate Your Goals and Dreams to God**
  Bring your goals, dreams, and ambitions before God in prayer. Committing them to Him shows that you trust Him to guide your steps and fulfill His purpose through you.

- **Reflect on Areas of Growth**
  Think about areas in your life where you can grow spiritually. Renewing your commitment often means letting go of

habits or attitudes that hinder your relationship with God.

- **Seek Accountability**
 Share your commitment with someone you trust. Accountability helps keep you focused and strengthens your resolve to stay true to your commitment.

- **Make Time for Daily Connection**
 Renewing your commitment includes making time each day to connect with God through prayer, worship, and Bible study. A consistent routine keeps you grounded in your faith.

- **Pray for Steadfastness**
 Ask God to help you stay true to your commitment, especially during challenging times. Pray for a heart that is fully devoted to following His will.

Dear God, I commit my plans, my dreams, and my life to You. Help me to renew my commitment every day and to grow closer to You. Strengthen my resolve to follow Your ways and establish my steps according to Your purpose.
In Jesus' Name, Amen.

Embracing God's Call

"Therefore, my dear brothers and sisters, stand firm. Let nothing move you. Always give yourselves fully to the work of the Lord, because you know that your labor in the Lord is not in vain." – 1 Corinthians 15:58

God calls each of us to a unique purpose, and embracing that call brings fulfillment and meaning to our lives. 1 Corinthians 15:58 encourages us to stand firm in our work for the Lord, knowing that it has eternal value. Embracing God's call involves dedication, courage, and a willingness to serve Him with all our heart.

- **Pray for Clarity in Your Calling**
  Spend time in prayer, asking God to clarify His purpose for you. Knowing your calling helps you stay focused and dedicated to the work He has set before you.

- **Serve Wholeheartedly**
  Whatever God calls you to do, give it your best. Serving wholeheartedly reflects your

commitment to God and your desire to honor Him.

- **Stay Faithful, Even in Small Tasks**
  Every task matters in God's plan, no matter how small. Embrace each opportunity as a chance to serve Him and make a difference.

- **Stand Firm Amid Challenges**
  Pursuing your calling can bring obstacles, but standing firm in faith keeps you rooted. Trust that God is with you and will provide strength for every challenge.

- **Pray for Strength and Dedication**
  Ask God for the strength to fulfill your calling and the dedication to keep going, even when it's hard. Pray for His guidance to stay true to His purpose.

Dear God, thank You for calling me to serve and for giving me a purpose. Help me to stand firm, embrace Your call, and serve You wholeheartedly. Give me strength and dedication to follow Your path, trusting that my work in You has eternal value.
In Jesus' Name, Amen.

Surrendering Your Will

"Father, if you are willing, take this cup from me; yet not my will, but yours be done." – Luke 22:42

Surrendering your will to God can be one of the hardest yet most freeing steps in your faith journey. Jesus, in the Garden of Gethsemane, demonstrated ultimate surrender when He prayed for God's will above His own. When we yield to God's plan, we acknowledge His wisdom and trust that His ways are best.

- **Let Go of Control**
  Acknowledge areas where you're holding onto control and invite God to take over. Surrendering to His will allows Him to work fully in your life.

- **Pray for Strength to Trust God's Plan**
  Like Jesus, ask God for strength to trust His plan, especially when it differs from your own desires. Trusting Him brings peace and assurance that He knows what's best.

- **Release Fears and Doubts**
  Surrendering includes letting go of fears that may be holding you back. Remember that God is in control, and His plans for you are good.

- **Reflect on Jesus' Example of Surrender**
  Jesus' willingness to submit to God's will, even in the face of suffering, serves as a powerful example. Look to His life for inspiration and courage to yield to God.

- **Pray for Complete Surrender**
  Ask God to help you release your own will and to give you a heart fully surrendered to His purpose. Surrendering allows God to guide and bless you in ways you may not expect.

---

*Dear God, help me to surrender my will to Yours, trusting that Your plan is always best. Give me the courage to release my own desires and to embrace Your purpose for my life. May I follow Jesus' example of obedience and yield to Your will in all things.
In Jesus' Name, Amen.*

Seeking God's Guidance Daily

"Trust in the Lord with all your heart and lean not on your own understanding; in all your ways submit to him, and he will make your paths straight."
– Proverbs 3:5-6

Trusting God daily is key to a strong, committed relationship with Him. Proverbs 3:5-6 teaches us to rely on God's wisdom rather than our own understanding. This requires a willingness to surrender control and trust in God's leading, even when we don't see the full picture. Making it a habit to seek His guidance each day allows us to stay grounded and aligned with His purpose.

- **Start Each Day in Prayer**
  Begin each morning by asking God for guidance and clarity. A simple prayer each day invites God to direct your steps and gives you the peace to trust His wisdom.

- **Trust Beyond Your Own Understanding**
  There may be times when you don't understand what God is doing. Choose to

trust Him, knowing that His ways are higher than ours and that He has a good plan for you.

- **Look for God's Hand in Every Situation**
As you go about your day, look for signs of God's presence and guidance. He may speak to you through others, a Bible verse, or even an unexpected event that brings clarity.

- **Keep an Open Heart**
Be open to the ways God might be guiding you. Sometimes His plans differ from what we expect, so keep a heart ready to follow wherever He leads.

- **Pray for Continued Guidance and Trust**
End each day by thanking God for His guidance, even in areas where you may not fully understand His plan. Trust that He is leading you toward what's best.

Dear God, thank You for being my constant guide. Help me to seek Your guidance every day and to trust You, even when I don't understand. Give me a heart that's open to Your direction and a mind that's willing to surrender my own plans. Lead me in Your paths, Lord, and help me rely fully on Your wisdom.
In Jesus' Name, Amen.

Staying Faithful in Small Things

"Whoever can be trusted with very little can also be trusted with much." – Luke 16:10

Faithfulness in small things lays a foundation for greater responsibility and blessings. Luke 16:10 reminds us that God values the small, everyday acts of faithfulness and stewardship. When we commit to doing even the little things well, God sees and honors our dedication. This discipline strengthens our character and prepares us for more significant opportunities in His kingdom.

- **Focus on Consistency**
  Make it a priority to be consistent in your responsibilities, no matter how small they may seem. Whether it's work, relationships, or your spiritual life, faithfulness in these areas reflects a heart committed to God.

- **Embrace Humble Tasks**
  Don't overlook or dismiss tasks that seem mundane or unimportant. God often uses

these moments to shape our character and build our faith.

- **Be Diligent with Your Resources**
  Steward your resources well, even in small ways. Managing your time, money, and skills wisely honors God and prepares you for greater responsibilities.

- **Celebrate Small Victories**
  Recognize and celebrate the small successes along your journey. Each one is a step forward and an opportunity to give thanks for God's faithfulness.

- **Pray for a Faithful Heart**
  Ask God to help you stay faithful in every area of your life. Pray for strength and diligence to fulfill your responsibilities with integrity and love.

Dear God, thank You for the opportunity to serve You in all things, big and small. Help me to be faithful in the small tasks You've entrusted to me, and let my heart be steadfast in honoring You. May I see every responsibility as a chance to grow in faith and to glorify You.
In Jesus' Name, Amen.

Living with an Eternal Perspective

"So we fix our eyes not on what is seen, but on what is unseen, since what is seen is temporary, but what is unseen is eternal." – 2 Corinthians 4:18

Living with an eternal perspective means focusing on what truly matters in God's kingdom rather than being consumed by temporary concerns. 2 Corinthians 4:18 calls us to set our sights on the unseen, eternal realities of God's promises. This perspective helps us prioritize our faith, relationships, and actions in ways that align with God's eternal purpose.

- **Value Spiritual Growth Over Material Success**
  Focus on growing closer to God rather than accumulating wealth or status. Spiritual growth has eternal value, while earthly things fade away.

- **Invest in Relationships**
  Spend time building meaningful relationships that encourage and uplift you in faith. These connections have lasting value and help you grow in love and understanding.

- **Be Generous with Your Time and Resources**
  Use your time and resources to bless others and further God's kingdom. Acts of generosity reflect a heart focused on eternity rather than temporary gains.

- **Stay Rooted in God's Promises**
  In moments of hardship, remember that this life is temporary and that God has promised an eternal hope. Trusting in His promises helps you endure and stay committed.

- **Pray for an Eternal Mindset**
  Ask God to keep your focus on what truly matters. Pray for wisdom to live each day in a way that honors His eternal purpose and brings glory to His name.

Dear God, thank You for the hope of eternity with You. Help me to live each day with an eternal perspective, valuing what truly matters and trusting in Your promises. May my life be focused on things that have lasting value, bringing You glory and drawing others closer to You.
In Jesus' Name, Amen.

ABOUT RODNEY JACKSON

Rodney Jackson is a licensed and ordained minister who has dedicated his life to preaching the gospel and empowering others. His journey hasn't been an easy one; after facing significant challenges, including serving 20 years behind bars, Jackson emerged with a renewed sense of purpose. He pursued personal growth through education and vocational training, which ignited his passion for the trucking industry.

Determined to overcome the stigma of his past, Jackson started his own trucking business with a mission of putting people first. Jackson is committed to guiding other formerly incarcerated individuals, helping them build sustainable businesses through Box Truck 365, alongside his business partner and team. In addition, Jackson is the founder of Finish Strong Ministries and lives in North Texas with his wife and family.

ABOUT BOX TRUCK 365

Box Truck 365 is an organization founded by trucking entrepreneurs dedicated to educating, training, and informing others by sharing our industry knowledge. Our mission is to make starting a trucking business accessible, empowering educators and entrepreneurs with the skills and information to succeed.

DEVOTIONALS AVAILABLE FROM BOX TRUCK 365

KINGDOM COMMERCE:
A Devotional Guide for Trucking Entrepreneurs

Part I: Laying the Foundation
This part focuses on setting up the basics of a faith-centered business, including developing a plan, legal setup, and brand-building.
- **Section 1**: Foundations of Faith and Business
- **Section 2**: Developing a Business Plan
- **Section 3**: Legal and Logistical Considerations
- **Section 4**: Building Your Brand

Part II: Managing and Growing the Business
This part covers daily operations, financial stewardship, and the resilience needed to navigate challenges. It emphasizes how to manage the business effectively and prepare for growth.
- **Section 5**: Operations and Management
- **Section 6**: Financial Stewardship
- **Section 7**: Perseverance and Resilience
- **Section 8**: Expanding Your Business

Part III: Sustaining Success and Giving Back
The part volume focuses on maintaining a balanced, ethical, and community-focused approach to business, providing guidance for long-term success and contributions beyond profit.
- **Section 9**: Maintaining Work-Life Balance
- **Section 10**: Ethical Business Practices
- **Section 11**: Giving Back and Community Involvement
- **Section 12**: Sustaining Long-Term Success
- **Section 13**: Reflection and Commitment

OTHER RESOURCES AVAILABLE FROM BOX TRUCK 365

Build Your Own Box Truck Business Blueprint: A Beginners Guide

~

NON-CDL BOX TRUCK TRAINING PROGRAM
(Correctional Education Series – for Inmates)
1000 - Self-Paced Learning: Achieve Your Goals
1010 - Transportation Business Overview
1020 - Business Setup
1030 - FMCSA & Government Compliance
1040 - Commercial Trucks
1050 - Truck Driver Readiness
1060 - Hauling Freight
1070 - Streams of Income
1080 - Dispatching
1090 - Managing Operations

~

And more…

Please
Rate and Review This Book on Amazon

Thank you for choosing this book!

If you found it helpful, inspiring, or informative, please consider leaving a review on Amazon.

You can leave a review, even if the book was purchased by someone else.

1. Locate the book on Amazon.com
2. Scroll Down to "Customer Reviews" section
3. Click "Write a Customer Review"

Review this product

Share your thoughts with other customers

(Write a customer review)
,

Your feedback supports our ministry.
It also helps others discover resources that could transform their lives.
Every review makes a difference in helping us grow and continue providing valuable insights. We're grateful for your support!

www.ingramcontent.com/pod-product-compliance
Lightning Source LLC
Chambersburg PA
CBHW031444210526
45464CB00005B/2322